CYBER SECURITY

HOW TO PROTECT YOUR BUSINESS

SVEN HIMILSBACH

CONTAINS 3 ADDITIONAL CHAPTERS INCLUDING "HOW TO DEAL WITH RANSOMWARE"

Table of Contents

From Author

Welcome to the comprehensive guide to cybersecurity in the era of IoT, remote work, and artificial intelligence. As the reliance on technology grows, it's more important than ever for organizations and individuals to prioritize their cybersecurity efforts. With 15 years of experience in the corporate world working for industry leaders, the author of this book provides a wealth of knowledge and expertise on the subject. This guide will help organizations understand the importance of cybersecurity, the current threat landscape, and the best practices for protecting their assets and data. From small organisations with employees working remotely to large corporations, the guide covers all aspects of modern cybersecurity, providing a solid foundation for organizations to build their own effective cybersecurity programs.

I hope you will find it informative and helpful.

Sven

Introduction to Cyber Security:

Cyber security refers to the measures and practices taken to protect internet-connected systems, including hardware, software, and sensitive information, from theft, damage, or unauthorized access.

1.1. Overview of Cyber Security:

In today's world, the internet has become an integral part of our lives and has transformed the way we interact, conduct business, and manage information. However, this increased reliance on technology has also made us more vulnerable to cyber threats such as hacking, malware, and data breaches. Cyber security helps to address these threats and keep our information and systems secure.

1.2. Importance of Cyber Security for Businesses:

Cyber security is crucial for businesses of all sizes and industries. With the increasing use of technology in the workplace, companies must take steps to protect their sensitive information and systems from cyber attacks. Neglecting cyber security can lead to data breaches, loss of confidential information, and damage to a company's reputation. By implementing strong cyber security measures, businesses can prevent these risks and ensure the protection of their assets.

1.3. Potential Consequences of Neglecting Cyber Security:

Neglecting cyber security can have serious consequences for businesses, including financial losses, loss of customer trust, and damage to a company's reputation. In addition, companies that are responsible for sensitive information, such as personal data and financial information, can face legal consequences if they fail to adequately protect this information from cyber threats. In a worst case scenario a business can simply go bust due to impact of cyberattack. By understanding the potential consequences of neglecting cyber security, businesses can better prioritize their efforts and resources towards protecting their assets and information.

1.4 When it comes to Cyber Security, think CIA!

The CIA Triad is a widely used model in cybersecurity and stands for Confidentiality, Integrity, and Availability.

- Confidentiality refers to the protection of sensitive information from unauthorized access. It ensures that sensitive data is only accessible by authorized individuals.

- Integrity means that the data is accurate and complete, and has not been tampered with. It ensures that data is not modified or deleted without proper authorization.

- Availability refers to ensuring that authorized individuals can access the data when needed. It means that the data is always accessible and usable when required. These three components work together to ensure the security of an organization's information systems and protect sensitive information from potential threats.

1.5 When it comes to Cyber Security, think PPT!

People, Process, and Technology triad is another widely used model in cybersecurity.

- People refer to the employees, users, and stakeholders of an organization. They play a critical role in protecting the organization's information systems by following best practices and being aware of potential security threats.

- Process refers to the policies, procedures, and guidelines that govern an organization's cybersecurity practices. This includes risk management, incident response, and recovery, and data protection.

- Technology refers to the hardware, software, and tools that organizations use to secure their information systems. This includes firewalls, intrusion detection systems, and encryption software.

The People, Process, and Technology triad works together to provide a comprehensive approach to cybersecurity and helps organizations to mitigate risks and prevent potential security incidents.

1.6. When it comes to Cyber Security think Risk, Vulnerability and Threat!

Risk refers to the likelihood of harm occurring, considering both the likelihood and the potential consequences. It is the product of the probability of a threat exploiting a vulnerability and the negative impact that exploitation would have.

Vulnerability refers to a weakness or gap in security measures that could be exploited by a threat. For example, an outdated software that is not patched creates a vulnerability that could be exploited by a hacker.

Threat refers to a potential cause of harm or danger, such as a cyber attack, malware, or natural disaster. Threats can take many forms, such as intentional (e.g. cyberattacks by malicious actors), accidental (e.g. human error), or natural (e.g. natural disasters).

In summary, risks are the potential consequences of the combination of vulnerabilities and threats. To manage cyber security risks, it is necessary to identify and prioritize threats and vulnerabilities, and then implement measures to mitigate or reduce them.

Essential Elements of Cyber Security

People
Employee Involvement in Cyber Security

Employee involvement in cyber security is a critical aspect of a comprehensive security program. This is because employees, who are often the first line of defense, can play a crucial role in protecting sensitive information and preventing security incidents. By being knowledgeable about potential cyber threats and adhering to best practices, employees can help prevent attacks or minimize their impact. This can include recognizing phishing scams, using strong passwords, and keeping software up-to-date. Additionally, employee training and awareness programs can help to keep employees informed and motivated to participate in the overall security of the organization. By making cyber security a shared responsibility, businesses can build a strong security culture that empowers employees to be vigilant in protecting the organization's sensitive information.

Awareness Training for Employees

Security awareness training for employees is an essential aspect of an organization's overall cyber security strategy. It helps to educate employees about potential cyber threats, and how they can play a role in preventing security incidents from occurring. The importance of regular and up-to-date security awareness training cannot be overstated, as the cyber threat landscape is constantly evolving and new threats are emerging. Best practices for security awareness training include making the training interactive and engaging, regularly testing employee knowledge with phishing simulations, and ensuring that the training covers the latest security threats and best practices for preventing them. Examples of exercises could include simulated phishing scams, password strength assessments, and interactive presentations on topics such as safe browsing habits and secure email practices. Overall, the goal of security awareness training is to empower employees to be active participants in maintaining the security of the organization.

Recognizing Phishing Scams

Recognizing phishing scams is a critical aspect of cyber security awareness training for employees. Phishing scams are fraudulent emails that impersonate legitimate organizations and try to trick individuals into revealing sensitive information such as login credentials, financial information, and other personal data. To recognize phishing scams, employees should keep in mind the following best practices:

1. Look out for unusual sender addresses: Phishing scams often use fake or disguised sender addresses, so it's important to be wary of emails from unknown or suspicious sources.
2. Check for spelling and grammar errors: Phishing scams often contain spelling and grammar mistakes, which can be a red flag that the email is not legitimate.
3. Watch out for urgency or fear-mongering: Phishing scams often use fear or urgency to pressure individuals into taking immediate action, such as clicking on a link or providing sensitive information.

4. Verify links before clicking: Before clicking on any links in an email, employees should hover over the link to see the actual URL and verify that it belongs to a legitimate source.
5. Report suspicious emails: Employees should report any suspicious emails to the appropriate authorities, such as the IT department or cybersecurity team, to allow for proper investigation.

Some examples of phishing scams include:
1. Emails that impersonate popular online services such as PayPal or Amazon and ask for login credentials or other sensitive information.
2. Emails that claim to be from a bank or financial institution and ask for account information or personal data.
3. Emails that offer a reward or prize and ask for sensitive information in order to claim it.

It is important for employees to be aware of these common phishing scams and to take appropriate precautions to protect themselves and their organizations from these types of cyber threats. Regular and up-to-date security awareness training can help employees stay informed and alert to the latest phishing scams.

Creating Strong Passwords

Creating strong passwords is a critical aspect of cyber security. Strong passwords protect sensitive information and prevent unauthorized access to accounts. When creating a strong password, the following factors should be considered:

- Length: Longer passwords are generally more secure than shorter ones. Aim for a password that is at least 12 characters long.

- Complexity: Use a mix of uppercase and lowercase letters, numbers, and symbols to create a more complex password. Avoid using easily guessable information, such as your name, date of birth, or address.

- Uniqueness: Avoid using the same password for multiple accounts. If a password is compromised in one place, an attacker will have access to multiple accounts.

There are several techniques that can be used to create strong passwords:

- Passphrases: A passphrase is a string of words that can be used as a password. The words should be random and not related to each other. For example, "apple-banana-carrot-dog" could be a passphrase.

- Password Managers: Password managers can generate strong, random passwords and store them securely. This way, users only have to remember one master password to access all of their accounts.

- Combination of Characters: A combination of random letters, numbers, and symbols can be used to create a strong password. For example, "A7b#C8d@E9f!" could be a strong password.

Examples of strong passwords:

fR3$hV3g3t@bLe
H0u$3p1t+!C0tt0nC@ndy
M0unt@inBik3R@c3

How to build a strong password like the above? This can be derived from an easy-to-remember sentence, poem, song, or quote. For example, "I love New York!" can be transformed into "ILOv3Ny!" by replacing letters with numbers and symbols and shortening the length. This type of password is easy to remember and also strong, as it consists of multiple words and contains a mix of letters, numbers, and symbols.

Additionally, taking the first letter of each word in a memorable phrase can also be an effective technique for creating a strong password. For example, the phrase "Take me to the moon" can be transformed into "Tmt2tM!", making it both easy to remember and strong.

It is important to note that no matter what technique is used to create a password, it should always be unique, and not reused for multiple accounts. Regular password changes are also recommended to maintain security.

Best Practices for Online Safety

To ensure online safety, employees should follow the following best practices: keep software and security tools up-to-date, avoid public Wi-Fi whenever possible, be cautious of links and attachments in emails and instant messages, use multi-factor authentication for online accounts, keep personal information private, and never reuse passwords for multiple accounts. Additionally, employees should also be aware of social engineering tactics and avoid falling for scams or phishing attempts. Organizations can provide regular awareness training and promote safe online practices to help employees protect themselves and their organization from online threats.

Employee monitoring

Employee monitoring is crucial in maintaining the security of an organization. By monitoring the actions of employees, companies can detect and prevent any security breaches that may occur due to human error or malicious intent. Employee monitoring can help identify any suspicious behavior, such as accessing sensitive information without authorization, sending sensitive data to unauthorized individuals, or using company systems for personal purposes. It can also help identify any weaknesses in security protocols and help improve the overall security posture of the organization. Regular monitoring can provide valuable insight into the security awareness and compliance of employees, allowing companies to address any gaps in training and reinforce best practices. By implementing employee monitoring, organizations can ensure the protection of their valuable data and intellectual property. Special attention should be paid to disgruntled employs and these members of staff who handle sensitive information. Most valuable tools for this type of mentoring will be DLP (Data Leak Prevention) systems and proxy servers. It is very important that the organisation has got the ability to revoke employees access. This process should be well known and documented. Another thing which mustn't be forgotten is the principle of least privilege, which states that employees should only have access to the information and systems they need to perform their job, should be applied to minimize the risk.

Process

Governance, Risk and Compliance

Cybersecurity Governance, Risk and Compliance (GRC) is a set of practices, policies, and guidelines that aim to ensure the protection of an organization's information and assets from cyber threats. It involves the alignment of security measures with an organization's overall risk management and regulatory compliance requirements. The main objectives of Cybersecurity GRC are to minimize the risk of cyber attacks, ensure that security policies and procedures are in place and followed, and meet regulatory requirements.

The process of Cybersecurity GRC starts with the identification and assessment of risks, followed by the implementation of appropriate security controls to mitigate those risks. It also involves regular monitoring and review of the security posture to ensure that it is effective and up to date. Organizations must also ensure that their employees are trained and aware of their responsibilities in maintaining the security of the organization's information and assets.

Compliance with regulations such as the General Data Protection Regulation (GDPR) and the Payment Card Industry Data Security Standard (PCI DSS) is a critical aspect of Cybersecurity GRC. These regulations dictate specific requirements for protecting sensitive information, such as personal data and payment card information, and organizations must demonstrate their compliance to avoid significant fines and reputational damage.

In conclusion, Cybersecurity GRC is an essential component of an organization's overall security strategy. It helps to minimize the risk of cyber attacks, ensure compliance with regulations, and maintain the confidentiality, integrity, and availability of information and assets.

Most important processes

7 Steps of Incident Response

Incident response is the process of handling a security breach or cyber attack. The 7 steps of incident response are as follows:

1. Preparation: This step involves creating an incident response plan, identifying critical systems and data, and designating a team responsible for handling security incidents. It is important to train the incident response team on how to handle various types of security incidents.
2. Identification: During this step, the incident response team detects and identifies the security breach. This is typically done by monitoring security logs and network traffic, as well as receiving alerts from security tools.
3. Containment: The goal of this step is to stop the spread of the breach and prevent further damage. This may involve disconnecting affected systems from the network, isolating compromised systems, or removing malware.
4. Analysis: In this step, the incident response team evaluates the extent and impact of the breach, and identifies the cause of the incident. This may involve conducting a forensic analysis, examining system logs, or reviewing network traffic.
5. Eradication: In this step, the incident response team removes the root cause of the breach and takes steps to prevent similar incidents from happening in the future. This may involve patching vulnerabilities, updating security software, or deploying new security tools.
6. Recovery: This step involves restoring normal operations and ensuring that all systems and data are back to their pre incident state. This may involve restoring from backups, re-establishing network connectivity, or reconfiguring security tools.
7. Lessons Learned: The final step of incident response is to document the events of the incident and identify areas for improvement. This may involve conducting a post-incident review, updating the incident response plan, or providing additional training to the incident response team. The goal of this step is to prevent similar incidents from happening in the future.

Basic disaster recovery plan

A simple disaster recovery plan should consist of the following steps:

1. Identify critical systems and data: Determine which systems and data are most critical for your organization to function and prioritize them for recovery.
2. Develop a backup and storage strategy: Implement a backup solution that includes regular backups of all critical systems and data and ensure that backups are stored off-site.
3. Test disaster recovery procedures: Regularly test disaster recovery procedures to ensure they work as intended and to identify any areas for improvement.
4. Assign roles and responsibilities: Assign clear roles and responsibilities for key personnel in the event of a disaster.
5. Establish communication plan: Develop a plan for communicating with employees, customers, and stakeholders during a disaster.
6. Develop an incident response plan: Create a plan that outlines the steps to be taken in response to a disaster, including steps to minimize damage, isolate the issue, and restore critical systems and data.
7. Regularly review and update plan: Regularly review and update the disaster recovery plan to ensure it remains relevant and up-to-date.

Remember, the goal of a disaster recovery plan is to ensure that your organization can quickly and effectively recover from a disaster and minimize the impact on business operations.

Recovery Best Practices are important guidelines to follow in order to effectively respond and recover from a cyber attack. They include the following steps:

1. Preparation: Prepare a detailed disaster recovery plan, including backup procedures and communication protocols, to minimize downtime and reduce the impact of a cyber attack.
2. Containment: Quickly contain the spread of the attack to prevent further damage. This may involve disconnecting infected systems, isolating the source of the attack, or implementing network firewalls to block traffic.
3. Analysis: Thoroughly analyze the attack to determine the cause, scope, and potential impact. This information can then be used to inform decisions about recovery strategies.
4. Data Backup and Restoration: Restore critical data from a secure backup. This may involve restoring an entire system or just specific files or data sets.
5. System Restoration: Rebuild and restore affected systems to their previous state, or to a known secure state. This may include reloading operating systems, reinstalling applications, and reconfiguring network settings.
6. Post-Incident Review: Conduct a review of the incident to identify areas for improvement in your response and recovery processes. This may include updating your disaster recovery plan, enhancing security measures, and providing additional training to employees.
7. Continuous Improvement: Continuously monitor and update your disaster recovery plan and security posture to ensure you are ready to respond and recover quickly in the event of a future cyber attack.

By following these recovery best practices, organizations can minimize downtime and minimize the impact of cyber attacks on their operations. It is important to regularly review and update these processes to ensure they remain effective in a rapidly changing threat landscape.

Risk Assessment is a critical process in Cybersecurity that helps organizations identify, prioritize, and manage potential threats to their systems and data. It involves evaluating the likelihood and impact of potential security incidents to determine the level of risk and determine the best course of action to minimize or mitigate that risk.
Here is a basic template for performing a Risk Assessment:

1. Identify assets: Identify the critical assets, systems, and data that need to be protected.

2. Threat identification: Identify potential threats to the assets, including both internal and external threats.
3. Vulnerability assessment: Evaluate the current state of security controls and identify any vulnerabilities that could be exploited by threats.
4. Impact assessment: Determine the potential impact of each identified threat on the assets and the organization as a whole.
5. Likelihood assessment: Evaluate the likelihood of each threat occurring, taking into account both the current threat landscape and the organization's specific risk profile.
6. Risk calculation: Calculate the overall risk for each threat by combining the impact and likelihood assessments.
7. Mitigation and management: Develop a plan to mitigate or manage the risks, including implementing new controls, enhancing existing controls, or accepting the risk.
8. Monitoring and review: Regularly review the risk assessment to ensure that it remains relevant and up-to-date, and monitor the implementation of the mitigation and management plan.

This template provides a basic structure for performing a Risk Assessment, but it is important to note that the process may vary depending on the size and complexity of the organization, as well as the specific security requirements and regulations that apply.

Vulnerability Management

Vulnerability management is the process of identifying, evaluating, and prioritizing vulnerabilities in an organization's systems and applications, and then implementing the appropriate measures to mitigate them. This process is critical in maintaining the security and integrity of an organization's information and technology assets. The steps involved in a typical vulnerability management process are as follows:
1. Scanning and Identification: Scan the organization's systems and applications for vulnerabilities, using tools such as vulnerability scanners, and identify any potential security risks.
2. Assessment and Prioritization: Evaluate the severity of each vulnerability and prioritize them based on the potential impact to the organization's systems and data.
3. Remediation and Mitigation: Develop and implement a plan to remediate or mitigate the vulnerabilities, based on the priority level assigned to each. This may involve installing patches, upgrading systems, or implementing additional security measures.
4. Verification and Testing: Verify that the remediation and mitigation measures have been effective in addressing the vulnerabilities and test the systems to ensure that they are secure.
5. Reporting: Report on the results of the vulnerability management process, including the number and types of vulnerabilities discovered, the actions taken to mitigate them, and any residual risks that remain.
6. Monitoring: Continuously monitor the systems and applications for new or previously unknown vulnerabilities and repeat the vulnerability management process as needed.

7. Review and Improvement: Regularly review and evaluate the vulnerability management process to identify areas for improvement, and implement changes to ensure that it remains effective and efficient.

A well-designed and executed vulnerability management process is an essential part of an organization's overall cybersecurity strategy, as it helps to minimize the risk of successful attacks and ensure the security and integrity of the organization's information and technology assets.

Technology

Importance of keeping your devices up-to-date

Keeping devices up-to-date is critical in maintaining strong cybersecurity. Software updates often include important security patches that fix vulnerabilities and prevent potential data breaches. Neglecting to keep software updated leaves devices open to exploits that can allow hackers to steal sensitive information, install malware, or take control of the system. Outdated systems can also pose a risk to the larger network, allowing threats to spread and negatively impacting business operations. Regular software updates help organizations stay ahead of potential security threats and provide peace of mind that sensitive data is protected. It is best practice to have a clear and automated process for updating all devices, including desktops, laptops, servers, mobile devices, and other endpoints including AV updates. This ensures that all systems are secure and running the latest security features.

Regular backups

Regular backups are critical to ensuring the safety and availability of data in the event of a disaster, cyber attack or hardware failure. Backups help organizations to recover quickly from data loss, minimize downtime and reduce the impact of a disaster on business operations. Here are some reasons why regular backups are important:
1. Protects against data loss: Regular backups protect against data loss from a variety of sources such as hardware failure, cyber attacks, human error and natural disasters.
2. Reduces downtime: Regular backups help organizations to recover quickly from a disaster, minimizing downtime and minimizing the impact on business operations.
3. Compliance: Regular backups are necessary for compliance with regulations such as HIPAA, PCI and Sarbanes-Oxley, which require organizations to keep copies of sensitive data.
4. Cost-effective: Regular backups can be a cost-effective way to protect against data loss, especially compared to the cost of data recovery or system restoration.
5. Easy recovery: Regular backups make it easy to recover data in the event of a disaster, as backups can be quickly restored to new hardware.

To ensure the effectiveness of a backup strategy, it is important to test backups regularly, store backups in a secure offsite location and have a plan in place for disaster recovery.

Additionally, it is important to keep backups up-to-date to ensure that recent changes are included in the backups.

Password management and password managers

Password management is a critical aspect of cyber security as passwords are often the first line of defense against unauthorized access to sensitive information. Using weak or easily guessable passwords, reusing passwords across multiple accounts, or writing down passwords can put an individual or organization at significant risk. To mitigate this risk, password management best practices must be followed.

One of the most effective ways to manage passwords is by using a password manager. A password manager generates and stores strong, unique passwords for each online account, and automatically logs you in to those accounts with a single master password. This makes it much easier to use strong, unique passwords for all accounts, which greatly reduces the risk of a password-related breach.

Additionally, password managers often include features such as password strength analysis, password sharing for teams, and security alerts for compromised passwords, which make it easier for individuals and organizations to stay on top of their password security.

Below are some popular free password managers:

1. Bitwarden (https://bitwarden.com)
2. LastPass (https://www.lastpass.com)
3. Dashlane (https://www.dashlane.com)
4. 1Password (https://1password.com)
5. KeePass (https://keepass.info)

It is important to research each one and compare their features before selecting one that fits your needs.

Endpoint protection

Endpoint protection is a critical aspect of cybersecurity that helps protect computer systems and devices connected to a network from various threats such as malware, viruses, and hacking attacks. These devices include laptops, desktops, smartphones, and tablets that access the network regularly.

The purpose of endpoint protection is to safeguard against unauthorized access, data theft, and malware infections that can cause harm to the network or the individual devices. An endpoint protection solution usually comprises of antivirus software, firewalls, and intrusion detection systems to provide multi-layered security.

Regular software updates and patching of operating systems, applications and firmware are critical to maintain endpoint security. Additionally, endpoint protection solutions should be configured to meet the specific needs of the organization, taking into account the threat landscape, network topology, and data privacy requirements.

Moreover, organizations should also enforce endpoint protection policies and provide regular training to employees to ensure that they understand the importance of keeping their devices secure and avoid potential security risks.

Antivirus (AV) software and Endpoint Detection and Response (EDR) software are two important tools used in cybersecurity to protect endpoints such as laptops, desktops, and mobile devices from cyber attacks.

Antivirus (AV) software is designed to detect and remove malicious software such as viruses, worms, and Trojan horses from the endpoints. It does this by scanning the endpoints for known malware and quarantining any suspicious files or code. AV software typically uses signature-based detection, which is a database of known malware, to identify and stop attacks. The advantage of AV software is that it is relatively low cost, easy to use and widely available. However, AV software can be limited in its ability to detect newer, unknown malware that has not yet been added to the database.

Endpoint Detection and Response (EDR) software is a more comprehensive solution that provides a higher level of protection against cyber attacks. EDR software combines traditional antivirus capabilities with advanced threat detection and response capabilities. It uses behavioral analysis, machine learning, and other techniques to detect malicious activity on endpoints, even if the malware is new and unknown. EDR software also provides incident response capabilities, allowing administrators to quickly respond to and remediate any cyber attacks.

The advantage of EDR software is its ability to detect and respond to advanced threats, but it can be more complex to set up and manage, and is typically more expensive than AV software.

Data Loss Prevention

Data Loss Prevention (DLP) is a cybersecurity solution that helps organizations to prevent sensitive information from being leaked, either accidentally or maliciously. The solution uses a set of policies, technologies, and processes to detect, monitor, and protect data in transit, at rest, or in use. DLP can be applied across different platforms, including email, cloud storage, file servers, endpoints, and more.
DLP can be based on different methods, such as content analysis, encryption, tokenization, and data masking. The goal of DLP is to identify and block sensitive information from leaving the organization, or to allow it to leave only in a controlled and secure manner. For example, DLP can prevent employees from emailing sensitive files to unauthorized recipients, uploading them to unsecured cloud storage, or copying them to removable devices.
The advantages of DLP include:
- Better protection of sensitive information: DLP helps to secure data that is critical to the organization's operations, reputation, and compliance obligations.

- Increased visibility and control: DLP provides real-time monitoring and reporting of data movements, which helps to identify potential security incidents and respond promptly.
- Better compliance with regulations: DLP helps to meet the requirements of various regulations, such as GDPR, HIPAA, PCI-DSS, and others, by ensuring that sensitive information is handled and processed appropriately.
- Improved data governance: DLP helps to enforce the organization's data policies and standards, and to ensure that sensitive information is used only for authorized purposes.

The disadvantages of DLP include:
- High implementation and maintenance costs: DLP solutions can be complex and require significant investment, both in terms of hardware, software, and staff.
- Interference with normal workflows: DLP can disrupt normal business processes, for example, by blocking emails, files, or websites that contain sensitive information.
- False positive and negative alarms: DLP can generate false alerts, either by identifying harmless data as sensitive or by missing real threats. This can result in increased workload for IT and security staff, and reduced trust in the solution.
- Increased complexity: DLP can increase the complexity of the security landscape, by adding another layer of protection, management, and reporting. This can also increase the risk of human error and misconfigurations.

Intrusion Detection and Prevention Systems

Intrusion Detection and Prevention Systems (IDPS) are security solutions designed to detect and prevent malicious activities on a computer network. The primary function of an IDPS is to analyze network traffic for signs of intrusion and malicious activities. This is achieved through the use of various techniques, including signature-based detection, anomaly detection, and behavior-based detection.

Signature-based detection involves identifying malicious activities based on predefined patterns, such as the signature of a virus or malware. Anomaly detection uses statistical analysis to identify behavior that deviates from the normal patterns of network traffic. Behavior-based detection uses machine learning algorithms to identify behavior patterns that are indicative of malicious activities.

IDPS solutions can be implemented in different ways, such as host-based IDPS (installed on individual endpoints), network-based IDPS (installed at the network perimeter), and cloud-based IDPS (hosted in the cloud). The benefits of IDPS solutions include improved security, reduced downtime, and faster detection and response times. However, IDPS solutions can also generate false positive alerts, which can lead to increased workload for security teams.

To be effective, IDPS solutions must be properly configured and maintained, and the security team must have the skills and knowledge necessary to interpret the alerts generated by the solution. Regular security assessments and threat hunting exercises can help organizations optimize their IDPS solutions and improve their overall security posture.

Multi-Factor Authentication (MFA) is an authentication method that requires multiple forms of authentication to be provided by a user in order to access a system or application. MFA combines multiple authentication factors, such as something a user knows (e.g. password or personal identification number), something a user has (e.g. smart card or security token) or something a user is (e.g. biometric authentication such as fingerprint or facial recognition). MFA is used as an additional layer of security to ensure that only authorized users can access sensitive information and systems. It is especially important for systems and applications that hold critical data, such as financial systems, healthcare systems, and government systems. By requiring multiple forms of authentication, MFA makes it much more difficult for an attacker to gain unauthorized access to these systems, even if the attacker has obtained the user's password.

Some common forms of MFA include SMS-based authentication, biometric authentication, and smart card or security token-based authentication. MFA can be implemented either through hardware-based devices or software-based solutions, depending on the level of security required.

To be effective, MFA must be implemented in a secure and user-friendly manner, with clear guidelines and procedures in place to ensure that users are aware of how and when to use MFA. MFA must also be supported by appropriate security policies, procedures and technologies to ensure that it is properly integrated into the overall security framework of the organization.

In summary, Multi-Factor Authentication is a critical component of any cyber security program, and provides a strong additional layer of security to protect sensitive information and systems from unauthorized access.

Data encryption

Data encryption is the process of converting plaintext data into a code to prevent unauthorized access. It is a critical aspect of cybersecurity and helps protect sensitive data in transit and at rest. In business, it is important to consider the following when deciding what should be encrypted:

1. Confidential data: This includes sensitive information such as financial records, customer data, and trade secrets.
2. Data in transit: Any data that is transmitted over the internet or other networks should be encrypted to prevent eavesdropping.
3. Data at rest: Encrypting data stored on servers, hard drives, and other storage devices can help protect against unauthorized access if the devices are lost or stolen.

Best practices for data encryption include using strong encryption algorithms, using encryption certificates from trusted sources, regularly changing encryption keys, and ensuring all encryption technologies are kept up to date. It is also important to have a comprehensive data backup and recovery plan in place in case the encrypted data needs to be recovered.

Technologies for monitoring workforce

Employee monitoring is a crucial aspect of cybersecurity, especially in organizations that handle sensitive information. There are various technologies that can be used to monitor employees, including proxy servers and software that takes regular screenshots of employee workstations.

A proxy server acts as an intermediary between an employee's device and the internet. It allows the organization to control access to websites, block certain content, and monitor employee activity. By using a proxy server, organizations can ensure that employees are not visiting malicious websites or downloading inappropriate content.
Software that takes regular screenshots of employee workstations can help organizations monitor employee activity and ensure that employees are using their devices for work-related tasks. This software can be programmed to take screenshots at specified intervals, providing organizations with a visual record of what employees are doing on their workstations.

It is important to note that employee monitoring should be subject to the employee's awareness and approval. Organizations should have clear policies in place that outline the types of monitoring that will take place, the purpose of the monitoring, and the consequences of not adhering to the policies.
In conclusion, employee monitoring is an important aspect of cybersecurity, and proxy servers and screenshot software are two of the technologies that can be used for monitoring employees. However, organizations should ensure that they have clear policies in place, and that employees are aware of the monitoring.

Internal WiFi protection

WiFi protection solutions refer to technologies and tools that are designed to secure wireless networks and protect them from cyber-attacks. One example of such a solution is Motorola Airdefence. This technology provides wireless intrusion prevention, wireless intrusion detection, wireless access control and wireless security reporting.
Motorola Airdefence works by monitoring the wireless network in real-time and detecting any suspicious or malicious activities. It identifies potential threats, such as unauthorized access, rogue access points, and network intrusions, and responds accordingly to prevent unauthorized access. Additionally, it provides a comprehensive set of security features, including encryption, authentication, and access control, to ensure the confidentiality, integrity and availability of data transmitted over the wireless network.

Using a WiFi protection solution like Motorola Airdefence provides several benefits, including:
- Improved network security: The solution helps to prevent unauthorized access to the network, reducing the risk of cyber-attacks, data theft, and other malicious activities.

- Increased visibility and control: A WiFi protection solution provides administrators with real-time visibility into the wireless network, enabling them to identify and resolve potential security issues quickly.
- Compliance with industry standards: Many WiFi protection solutions are designed to meet industry standards, such as PCI DSS, HIPAA, and others, helping organizations to comply with regulatory requirements.
-

In conclusion, using a WiFi protection solution like Motorola Airdefence can provide a comprehensive layer of security for wireless networks, helping organizations to prevent cyber-attacks, improve network visibility and control, and comply with industry standards.

Honeypots

Honeypot is a security technique that involves setting up a fake network or system to attract and trap potential attackers or malware. The idea behind this technique is to distract the attackers away from the actual target and to gather information about the attacker's methods and tools. This information can then be used to improve the overall security posture and to detect and respond to future attacks.

Honeypots can be used to detect unauthorized access, gather intelligence about attacker techniques, and track malicious activity. For example, a honeypot can be used to simulate a vulnerable network service, like a web server, or to imitate a user's email account. If an attacker interacts with the honeypot, security professionals can then use the information gathered to strengthen their defenses and to track the attacker's movements.

There are different types of honeypots, ranging from low-interaction honeypots that simulate limited parts of a system to high-interaction honeypots that are designed to imitate an entire operating system. It is important to note that honeypots should not be the only security technique used, but rather they should be used in conjunction with other security measures, such as firewalls and intrusion detection systems.

Overall, honeypots are a valuable tool for organizations looking to detect and respond to cyber attacks. They provide an opportunity to gather valuable intelligence about attackers and their methods, which can be used to improve the overall security posture and to protect against future attacks.

Data integrity solutions

Data integrity solutions, such as Tripwire, ensure that data within a system remains unchanged and is protected from tampering. Tripwire is a security solution that monitors, detects, and alerts on changes to critical system files and configurations. The solution uses checksum algorithms to verify the integrity of system files, configurations, and other important data, allowing administrators to quickly identify any unauthorized changes.
The key advantage of Tripwire and other data integrity solutions is the ability to detect and prevent data tampering, which can cause harm to a system and its users. This includes unauthorized changes made by attackers, as well as accidental changes made by system

administrators. Data integrity solutions can also help organizations comply with regulations and standards that require maintaining the authenticity and confidentiality of sensitive data. Another benefit of Tripwire is the ability to automate the monitoring and reporting process, saving time and resources for IT and security teams. The solution also provides detailed audit trails and reports, making it easier to track changes and resolve issues.

In conclusion, Tripwire and other data integrity solutions are an essential component of a comprehensive cybersecurity strategy. They help organizations maintain the integrity of their data, prevent data tampering, and comply with regulations and standards.

Safety using Public Wi-Fi

Public Wi-Fi networks are often used to access the internet in public places such as coffee shops, airports, hotels, and parks. They can be convenient and save data on your mobile plan, but they also come with security risks. To ensure safe use of public Wi-Fi, consider the following best practices:

1. Avoid Sensitive Transactions: Avoid accessing sensitive information like banking accounts, personal data, and company data on public Wi-Fi networks.
2. Use a VPN: A Virtual Private Network (VPN) encrypts your internet traffic, making it difficult for hackers to intercept your data.
3. Watch Out for Phishing: Be careful of fake Wi-Fi networks set up by hackers, who then use phishing tactics to steal your login credentials.
4. Update Software Regularly: Make sure your device's software and anti-virus are up to date, as older versions may contain vulnerabilities that hackers can exploit.
5. Disable Sharing: Disable file and printer sharing on your device when using public Wi-Fi to reduce the risk of unauthorized access.
6. Use a Strong Password: If you need to access Wi-Fi networks that require a password, make sure to use a strong, unique password.

By following these best practices, you can reduce the risk of cyber attacks and ensure the safety of your data when using public Wi-Fi networks.

Additional considerations

Third party security risks and mitigation

Third-party security risks refer to the potential threats to an organization's data and systems posed by external vendors and partners. These risks can arise from the use of third-party software, cloud services, or any other technology that integrates with an organization's infrastructure. The consequences of a security breach caused by a third party can be severe, including loss of sensitive data, damage to reputation, and financial losses.

To mitigate third-party security risks, organizations should follow best practices in due diligence, risk assessment, and contract negotiation. During the due diligence phase, organizations should conduct thorough background checks on potential third-party partners, including reviewing their security policies and procedures. This can be done by requesting security questionnaires or on-site assessments.

When conducting a risk assessment, organizations should identify potential security threats and assess the impact that a breach caused by a third-party would have on their operations. It is also important to consider the sensitivity of the data that will be shared with the third party and the level of access they will have to the organization's systems.

Finally, contract negotiation is an important step in mitigating third-party security risks. Organizations should ensure that contracts with third-party vendors clearly define security expectations and responsibilities, including the requirement for regular security audits, security breach reporting, and the use of encryption. Additionally, contracts should specify the actions that will be taken in the event of a security breach, such as termination of the agreement and notification of affected individuals.

To summarize, mitigating third-party security risks requires a comprehensive approach that includes due diligence, risk assessment, and contract negotiation. By following these best practices, organizations can reduce the risk of a security breach and protect their sensitive data and systems.

Cyber Security for Remote Workers

Cyber security for remote workers is an important aspect of an organization's overall security strategy, as an increasing number of employees are working from home due to the pandemic and other reasons. It requires a comprehensive approach to ensure the protection of sensitive data and information, as remote workers may not have the same level of security as office workers.

Here are some best practices for securing remote workers:
1. Provide secure remote access: Offer secure access methods, such as Virtual Private Network (VPN) or Secure Shell (SSH) to ensure that remote workers have a secure connection to the organization's network.
2. Enforce strong password policies: Require remote workers to use strong and unique passwords, and enforce multi-factor authentication for all remote access methods.
3. Implement device management: Ensure that remote workers are using approved and secure devices, such as laptops and smartphones, and install security software, such as anti-virus and firewall, on all devices.
4. Regularly update software: Ensure that remote workers are using the latest software and security patches, as out-of-date software can be exploited by attackers.
5. Encrypt data: Encrypt sensitive data that is transmitted or stored on remote devices, such as financial information or personal data, to prevent unauthorized access.
6. Provide training: Regularly train remote workers on cyber security best practices, such as avoiding phishing scams and keeping their software up-to-date.
7. Monitor activity: Monitor remote worker activity to detect any suspicious activity, such as unauthorized access to sensitive information.

In conclusion, securing remote workers requires a comprehensive approach, including secure remote access, strong passwords, device management, software updates, encryption, training, and monitoring. By implementing these best practices, organizations can reduce the risk of cyber security threats and protect their sensitive data and information.

Importance of Physical Security in relation to Cyber Security

Physical security plays a crucial role in overall cybersecurity. Physical devices such as servers, storage devices, and workstations store sensitive information and host critical systems, so it is essential to secure these devices from theft, damage, or unauthorized access. Physical security measures, such as locking doors, restricting access to server rooms, using surveillance cameras, and using fire suppression systems, can help prevent malicious actors from accessing these devices.

Additionally, physical security measures such as secure disposal of devices can help prevent sensitive information from falling into the wrong hands. For example, when disposing of hard drives, it is important to erase the data completely to prevent sensitive information from being recovered.

Physical security is especially important for organizations that handle sensitive information, such as personal information or financial data, or that operate critical infrastructure systems. By securing physical devices, organizations can reduce the risk of data breaches, unauthorized access, and other cybersecurity incidents.
In summary, physical security is an integral part of overall cybersecurity and should not be overlooked. Organizations should assess their physical security measures regularly and take steps to ensure that they are adequately protected.

Threat Intelligence

Cyber Threat Intelligence (CTI) is a proactive approach to understanding and anticipating the evolving threat landscape. CTI aims to provide organizations with information about known and emerging threats, enabling them to take steps to mitigate the risks. The purpose of CTI is to provide relevant and actionable information to organizations about threats, enabling them to make informed decisions about risk management and incident response.

CTI is typically used by organizations as part of their overall security program, to enhance their situational awareness and help them respond effectively to potential threats. The information collected by CTI may be used to develop threat intelligence reports, alerts, and notifications that provide organizations with real-time information about emerging threats. There are many free resources available to organizations looking to obtain CTI. Here are some of the best free sources:
Threat Intelligence Platforms: Offered by organizations such as Anomali, ThreatConnect, and the Cyber Threat Alliance, these platforms provide a centralized repository for threat intelligence information, including indicators of compromise, intelligence feeds, and vulnerability information.
Anomali: https://www.anomali.com/platform
ThreatConnect: https://www.threatconnect.com/platform/
Cyber Threat Alliance: https://cyberthreatalliance.org/

Threat Intelligence Feeds: Threat intelligence feeds provide organizations with real-time information about emerging threats. Some free feeds include the Open Threat Exchange (OTX) and the VirusTotal Intelligence Service.
Open Threat Exchange (OTX): https://otx.alienvault.com/
VirusTotal Intelligence Service: https://www.virustotal.com/intelligence/

Government Websites: Many government organizations, such as the Department of Homeland Security (DHS) and the Federal Bureau of Investigation (FBI), provide free threat intelligence information to organizations. For example, the DHS has a Cybersecurity and Infrastructure Security Agency (CISA) that provides organizations with a wide range of cybersecurity-related information.
Department of Homeland Security (DHS): https://www.dhs.gov/
Federal Bureau of Investigation (FBI): https://www.fbi.gov/
Cybersecurity and Infrastructure Security Agency (CISA): https://www.cisa.gov/

Community-Based Threat Intelligence: Many communities, such as the SANS Internet Storm Center, the ISC Handler's Diary, and the Cyber Threat Alliance, provide organizations with free threat intelligence information. These communities often rely on contributions from volunteers and members to gather and share information about emerging threats.
SANS Internet Storm Center: https://isc.sans.edu/
ISC Handler's Diary: https://isc.sans.edu/diary/
Cyber Threat Alliance: https://cyberthreatalliance.org/

Industry Specific ISACs: Certain industries have their own Information Sharing and Analysis Centers (ISACs), such as the Financial Services ISAC (FS-ISAC), which provides financial organizations with real-time information about threats specific to their industry.
Financial Services ISAC (FS-ISAC): https://www.fsisac.com/

Cyber Security News and Blogs:

The register: https://www.theregister.com/Tag/Cybersecurity/
The hacker news: https://thehackernews.com/

Examples of Country Specific Compliance and Regulations

Cybersecurity country specific compliance and regulations refer to the laws and regulations that organizations must abide by in order to secure sensitive information and protect the privacy of individuals. Examples of such regulations include:
1. General Data Protection Regulation (GDPR): This regulation is applied in the European Union and requires organizations to protect the personal data of individuals. Organizations must report data breaches within 72 hours and enforce strict data protection measures.
2. Information Commissioner's Office (ICO): This is a regulatory body in the United Kingdom responsible for upholding information rights and protecting the privacy of individuals. The ICO provides guidance on data protection and has the power to enforce penalties for organizations that breach data protection laws.

3. California Consumer Privacy Act (CCPA): This regulation is applied in California, United States and gives California residents the right to know what data organizations are collecting about them, the right to request deletion of that data, and the right to opt out of the sale of their data.
4. Japan's Act on the Protection of Personal Information (APPI): This regulation is applied in Japan and requires organizations to take measures to protect personal information and implement procedures to prevent unauthorized access and unauthorized disclosure.

It's important for organizations to be aware of the specific regulations that apply to them, as non-compliance can result in significant fines and reputational damage. It's recommended to consult with a legal professional to understand the specific requirements and ensure compliance.

Bonuses

How to check if a URL is malicious?

Checking if a URL is malicious is a crucial step in ensuring your online security and avoiding the risks of malware and other malicious activities. Here are some resources you can use to determine if a website is malicious:

urlscan.io: urlscan.io is a free online service that analyzes and checks the security of a URL. It provides information on the URL's content, IP addresses, and domains, among other things. It also gives you a detailed report on the potential risks of a website, including malware, phishing, and other malicious activities.
URL: https://urlscan.io/

Joesandbox: Joesandbox is a free online tool that analyzes the behavior of a website to determine if it's malicious. It provides a detailed report on the website's behavior and activities, including the processes it runs, the files it creates, and the network activity it generates.
URL: https://joesandbox.com/

VirusTotal: VirusTotal is a free online service that allows you to check if a URL or file is malicious. You can enter a URL or upload a file to VirusTotal, and it will perform a thorough analysis to determine if it's safe or not. It analyzes the file using multiple antivirus engines to provide a comprehensive report on the potential risks.
URL: https://www.virustotal.com/

Note: It's important to keep in mind that no single tool can guarantee 100% protection against malicious websites, and it's always advisable to exercise caution when visiting unfamiliar websites.

Ransomware is a type of malicious software that encrypts the victim's files and demands payment in exchange for the decryption key. Dealing with ransomware can be a challenging and time-sensitive task, but following best practices can help organizations mitigate the risk of a ransomware attack and reduce the impact if one occurs. Here are some best practices for dealing with ransomware:

1. Backup Regularly: Regular backups of critical data and systems are essential for quickly recovering from a ransomware attack. Organizations should store backups off-site or in the cloud to ensure that they are not affected by the attack.
2. Use Antivirus and Endpoint Protection: Installing and regularly updating antivirus software and endpoint protection systems can help prevent ransomware from infecting a system.
3. Implement Network Segmentation: Network segmentation can limit the spread of ransomware within a network by isolating infected systems from the rest of the network.
4. Keep Software Up-to-Date: Keeping all software up-to-date, including operating systems, applications, and browsers, helps reduce the risk of a successful ransomware attack.
5. Educate Employees: Employee education is critical in preventing a ransomware attack. Employees should be trained on how to identify phishing emails, avoid downloading suspicious files, and report any suspicious activity.
6. Monitor Network Traffic: Monitoring network traffic can help detect a ransomware attack in progress and allow organizations to respond quickly.
7. Have a Response Plan: Organizations should have a well-documented response plan in place in case of a ransomware attack. This plan should include procedures for containing the attack, restoring systems, and communicating with stakeholders.
8. Do Not Pay the Ransom: While paying the ransom may seem like the quickest solution, it is not recommended. Paying the ransom not only encourages the attackers but also does not guarantee that the encrypted files will be decrypted.
9. Report the Attack: Reporting the attack to the appropriate authorities, such as law enforcement, can help track down the attackers and prevent future attacks.
10. Review and Improve: After a ransomware attack, organizations should review their security posture and make improvements to prevent future attacks. This may include implementing additional security measures, updating policies, and retraining employees.

By following these best practices, organizations can reduce the risk of a ransomware attack and minimize the impact if one occurs.

Glossary – useful Cyber Security terminology

A -

- Access Control: The process of limiting access to resources based on an authorization policy
- Authentication: The process of verifying the identity of a user or device
- Antivirus Software: A software application that helps protect a computer or network from malicious software such as viruses, worms, Trojans, and spyware
- Asymmetric Encryption: A type of encryption that uses two keys, one for encryption and one for decryption, to ensure secure communication

B -

- Backup: A copy of data that is stored in a separate location, in case the original data is lost or becomes unavailable
- Botnet: A group of compromised computers that are controlled by a cybercriminal to carry out malicious activities
- Bytecode: A compiled version of a program that is executed by a virtual machine, rather than the computer's hardware

C -

- Cipher: An algorithm used to encrypt and decrypt data
- Cloud Computing: A model of delivering IT services over the internet
- Cold Site: A type of disaster recovery site that has the infrastructure in place to recover IT systems, but no data or equipment
- Cyber Attack: A deliberate attempt by a cybercriminal to damage, disrupt, or steal data from a computer system or network

D -

- Data Backup: A copy of data that is stored in a separate location, in case the original data is lost or becomes unavailable
- Data Encryption: The process of converting data into a secret code to protect it from unauthorized access
- Data Loss Prevention (DLP): A technology that helps protect sensitive data by preventing it from being transferred outside of an organization
- Denial-of-Service (DoS) Attack: An attack that aims to make a computer resource unavailable to its intended users

E -

- Encryption: The process of converting data into a secret code to protect it from unauthorized access
- Endpoint: A device, such as a computer, smartphone, or tablet, that is used to access a network or the internet
- Endpoint Protection: A security solution designed to protect endpoints from various types of cyber attacks
- Ether: A cryptocurrency and blockchain platform that is used to build decentralized applications

F -

- Firewall: A security device that monitors incoming and outgoing network traffic and allows or blocks access based on a set of security rules
- Forensics: The process of collecting, analyzing, and preserving digital evidence for use in a legal or administrative investigation

G -

- Gateway: A device that acts as an intermediary between two networks, such as a local area network (LAN) and the internet
- Grayware: Software that is not malicious, but may cause problems or display unwanted behavior

H -

- Hash: A fixed-length output created from a variable-length input, using a mathematical function, that is used to verify the integrity of data
- Honeypot: A decoy system that is set up to lure in potential attackers and monitor their activities
- HTTPS: A protocol that provides secure communication over the internet, by encrypting data and validating the identity of the website

I -

- Incidence Response Plan: A documented set of procedures and guidelines for responding to a cyber attack or data breach.
- Incident Response Team (IRT): A group of individuals within an organization who are responsible for responding to and managing cyber incidents.
- Information Security: The practice of protecting information and information systems from unauthorized access, use, disclosure, disruption, modification, or destruction.
- Information System: A collection of hardware, software, data, and people used to create, process, store, and exchange information.
- Intrusion Detection System (IDS): A software system that automatically identifies and alerts on unauthorized access or security threats to a computer system or network.

J

- Junkware: Software that displays unwanted or irrelevant advertisements, such as pop-ups, banners, or interstitials.

K

- Key Logger: A software or hardware device used to monitor and record every keystroke entered on a computer or device.

L

- Logic Bomb: A piece of code that is programmed to perform a malicious action when certain conditions are met, such as a specific date or time.
- Log Management: The process of collecting, analyzing, and storing log data from various sources, such as firewalls, servers, and applications.
- Loss Prevention: Measures taken to prevent the loss or theft of information or other valuable assets.

M

- Malware: Short for "malicious software," this term refers to any software that is intentionally designed to harm or exploit computer systems.
- Man-in-the-Middle Attack: A type of cyber attack where an attacker intercepts communication between two parties and can read, modify, or inject messages into the conversation.
- Multi-Factor Authentication (MFA): A security process that requires multiple forms of authentication, such as a password and a fingerprint or a security token, to access an information system.

N

- Network: A group of interconnected computer systems or devices that can communicate with each other.
- Network Security: Measures taken to protect the confidentiality, integrity, and availability of information transmitted over a network.

O

- Online Fraud: A type of fraud that is committed using the Internet, such as phishing scams, e-commerce fraud, and social engineering attacks.
- Open-Source Intelligence (OSINT): Information gathered from publicly available sources, such as news articles, social media, and public databases.

P

- Phishing: A type of cyber attack where an attacker uses a fake website, email, or other form of communication to trick a victim into disclosing sensitive information, such as usernames and passwords.
- Policy: A set of rules and guidelines that govern how an organization manages information security and privacy.
- Penetration Testing: A simulated cyber attack on a computer system or network to test its security posture and identify vulnerabilities.
- Privacy: The right of individuals to control how their personal information is collected, used, and disclosed.

Q

- Quarantine: A security measure used to isolate potentially malicious files or devices from a network to prevent further spread of malware or other security threats.

R

- Ransomware: A type of malware that encrypts a victim's data and demands payment in exchange for the decryption key.
- Risk: The potential for harm or damage to occur as a result of a security threat.
- Risk Management: The process of identifying, assessing, and prioritizing risks to an organization and implementing measures to mitigate those risks.

S

- Sandbox: A virtual environment where malware or other potentially harmful code can be executed and observed without posing a threat to the underlying system.
- Security: Measures taken to protect systems, devices, and data from unauthorized access, damage, or theft.
- Security Awareness Training: A type of training that teaches employees about security best practices and how to identify and respond to cyber threats.
- Social Engineering: A type of attack that uses psychological manipulation to trick victims into revealing sensitive information or performing actions that compromise security.
- Spam: Unsolicited or unwanted electronic messages, often sent in bulk and containing advertisements or malicious links.
- Spyware: A type of malware that surreptitiously collects and transmits sensitive information from an infected device.
- System Hardening: The process of securing an operating system or application by removing unnecessary components, updating software, and configuring security settings.

T

- Threat: A potential security risk or vulnerability that could be exploited by attackers.

- Threat Intelligence: Information about known and emerging cyber threats that can be used to improve security posture and decision-making.
- Two-Factor Authentication (2FA): An authentication process that requires the user to provide two forms of identification, such as a password and a security token.

U

- Unix: A family of operating systems commonly used in servers and other large computer systems.
- URL (Uniform Resource Locator): The address of a specific web page or other internet resource.
- User Account: A set of permissions and settings that define what a user can do on a computer or network.

V

- Virus: Malicious software that infects a computer, spreads from one computer to another, and interferes with the normal functioning of a computer system.
- Vulnerability: A weakness in a computer system, application, or device that can be exploited by an attacker to cause harm or gain unauthorized access.

W

- WAF (Web Application Firewall): A security device or software that monitors incoming and outgoing network traffic and applies a set of rules to protect web applications from various threats.
- Worm: Malicious software that propagates itself over a network without requiring intervention from a user.

X

- XSS (Cross-Site Scripting): A type of security vulnerability that allows an attacker to inject malicious code into a web page viewed by other users.

Z

- Zero-Day: A vulnerability that is unknown to the vendor and is being actively exploited by attackers. The name refers to the number of days that the vendor has had to address the issue.
- Zombie Computer: A computer that has been compromised by malware and is controlled remotely by an attacker. The attacker can use the computer to launch attacks, spread malware, or conduct other malicious activities.

www.ingramcontent.com/pod-product-compliance
Lightning Source LLC
LaVergne TN
LVHW022127060326
832903LV00063B/4807